Achieving the
EXECUTION
EDGE™

20 Essential Questions Corporate Directors Need To Get Answered About Strategy Execution

Achieving the
EXECUTION
EDGE ™

**20 Essential Questions
Corporate Directors Need
To Get Answered About
Strategy Execution**

Chris Bart, Ph.D., FCPA and Elliot S. Schreiber, Ph.D.
Co-Founders of The Directors College of Canada

Published by
Bart & Company, Inc.
1063 King Street West
Suite 230
Hamilton, Ontario L8S4S3
Canada

Schreiber & Company
924 Bergen Avenue
Suite 202
Jersey City, NJ 07306

Manufactured in the United States of America, or in the United Kingdom when distributed elsewhere.

Bart, Chris, Ph.D., FCPA and Elliot S. Schreiber, Ph.D.
        Achieving the Execution Edge™

ISBN:
Print: 978-1-937504-59-5
Ebook: 978-1-937504-60-1
Library of Congress Control Number: 2013909385
Worthy Shorts ID: SBG101

Cover design by: Darlene Swanson • www.van-garde.com
Interior design: Darlene Swanson • www.van-garde.com

What Leading Corporate Directors Are Saying About This Publication...

"A critical contribution to directors' understanding of their oversight role in strategy execution, without crossing the line into management. This is a must read for every director who is serious about helping his company overcome the #1 impediment to organizational success."

Steve Odland, CEO, The Committee for Economic Development
Former Chairman & CEO, Office Depot, Former Chairman &
CEO, AutoZone, Director, General Mills
Former Chair, Business Roundtable
USA

"As a long time student of corporate organizational behavior and a veteran turn-around CEO and a director or former director of 20 or so organizations, I feel *Achieving the Execution Edge™: 20 Essential Questions Corporate Directors Need to Get Answered about Strategic Execution* addresses critical material lacking in the knowledge of many executives and directors. It not only addresses the basic question of "How" but it also both gives directors permission to probe this way, AND indicates that if they do not, they will not fully be discharging their fiduciary duties. I loved it all. *Achieving the Execution Edge™* is beautifully framed and every word is meaningful."

Deborah Hicks Midanek, President, Solon Group, Inc.
Chairman, Prevail Fund, Inc., USA

"A brilliant practice manual which will provide an invaluable service for each Director on how he can and should enhance their organization's ability to execute the strategy. By this manual, theory becomes practical! This is what we Directors have been waiting for!"

Joachim Rabe, Group CFO & Board Member,
Heristo AG
Germany

"In a world where directors are being increasingly held accountable for performance, this publication provides an essential practical guide to take a board from knowing the importance of strategy execution to being able to do it well in their organization."

Angela Pankhurst, Non-Executive Director, Chair,
Audit Committee
PanTerra Gold Ltd
Australia

"This is a concise, clear and very logical analysis of a recommended approach to the oversight of the execution of a corporate strategy. While every director knows that corporate strategy is critical to success, not all directors know and apply a methodical approach to overseeing the execution of an approved strategy. This book provides a lot of thoughtful insight into how directors may fulfill this responsibility."

John Manley, PC, OC
President & CEO, Canadian Council of Chief Executives
Former Deputy Prime Minister of Canada
Canada

"Drs. Chris Bart's and Elliot S. Schreiber's *Achieving the Execution Edge*™ is easy to understand and at the same time rigorous. It is mandatory reading for the chief executive, managing director, senior HR officer, COO, CRO, external board advisor, and, perhaps most importantly, non-executive director and board chair. Strategy applies to all companies, in any sector. It is the one area that is often addressed last by boards, well after oversight and compliance, but has the single greatest effect on an organization thriving, or even surviving. This book is well organized, covers all aspects of strategy, and has many practical appendices, tools, cases and takeaways. It is current and relevant, covering emerging issues such as social communication, incentives, risk, talent, total rewards, integration, and IT, as well as all traditional business and stakeholder processes and controls, including excellent chapters on the governance of strategic execution. The checklists and frameworks cover inception, design, all the way to implementation and follow up. I intend for this to be mandatory reading for my students and executives and directors I train, and it should be for anyone with strategic responsibility or oversight. I highly recommend this practical book."

Richard Leblanc, Ph.D.
Associate Professor, Law, Governance & Ethics York University
Canada

"Chris Bart and Elliot S. Schreiber have done an excellent job in providing specific and practical guidance to boards on how to help ensure that strategic plans are executed successfully. The breadth of coverage is comprehensive and is organized for easy reference on particular topics. This guide should be invaluable for directors of all sizes and types of organizations. There is so much literature out there that leaves you feeling unable to implement what you have read, while this has all the essentials together in a tidy package showing how to be a more effective board. It is honest, well written and based on practical experience as to what works and what doesn't. Essential reading for any board member."

John, R. S. Fraser, FCA
Chief Risk Officer, Hydro One
Canada

"*Achieving the Execution Edge*™: *20 Essential Questions Corporate Directors Need to Get Answered about Strategic Execution* provides a clear and compelling message about the important link between strategy and risk management. It also sheds light on the heretofore-blind spot that many organizations often overlook — the impact that culture has on how strategy gets implemented. These insights, together with many others, should be viewed as priorities of the first order for all board directors who now face increasingly higher standards of corporate governance."

Lloyd Komori
Chair, Governance & Nominating Committee
Toronto Central Local Health Integration Network
Managing Director, KCI Inc.
Canada

"With ongoing business and organizational failures, the same cannot continue. Research clearly shows the execution is critical and Board oversight of strategy execution is now part of the "new world order" for Directors. This excellent book clearly aims to assist you as a Director to drill into the how to ensure excellence in strategy execution."

Jason Masters
Director, Non-Executive Director,
Audit & Committee Chair & Member
Australia

"Simply put, corporate governance should be primarily about maximizing company performance and shareholder value. As an experienced non-executive chairman in multiple board restructuring situations and as an active/activist investor, I have clearly seen the significant lack of engagement on the part of boards in the overall value creation process. This is especially glaring in the lack of rigor applied to execution. Chris Bart and Elliot Schreiber have provided a clear and succinct road map that covers every essential element of execution. Theirs is a prescription not just for the boards of underperforming and undervalued companies, but for any board that chooses to set their sights on developing the full potential of the company they govern. This book should become a business classic."

Henry D. Wolfe
Chairman
De La Vega Occidental & Oriental Holdings
USA

"The simpler you are, the clearer it is to your audience."

—Charles Durning, Actor

"Simplify, simplify, simplify."

—Henry David Thoreau, *Walden Pond*

"The simplest explanation for some phenomenon is more likely to be accurate than more complicated explanations."

—*A variation on Occam's Razor*
(*"Pluralitas non est ponenda sine neccesitate"*)

Table of Contents

THE 20 ESSENTIAL QUESTIONS

Strategy

Communication and Awareness

Integration

Culture and Risk

Capability

Accountability and Recognition

Board Specific Execution Activities

Post Script Question:

How To Use This Publication

THIS PUBLICATION is designed to be a concise, easy-to-read introduction to the role that Directors play in performing one of their most important functions — *monitoring the execution of their organization's strategy.*

The question format of this publication reflects the oversight role of Directors, which includes asking management — and themselves — questions to fulfill their fiduciary and statutory responsibilities.

Unfortunately, in the past, not all Directors felt comfortable in asking questions in the boardroom, often because they did not know what types of questions to ask, or which ones were even permissible. Accordingly, the questions presented here offer guidance to corporate Directors on frameworks, processes and outcomes in order both to provide them with insight and to stimulate discussion on the important issues related to *strategy execution.*

These questions, however, are not intended to be a comprehensive checklist—they are merely a starting point. *But, they are questions for which the answers should be sought and known by every corporate Director.*

It should be pointed out that asking these questions directly of management may not always be the preferred course of action. In such circumstances, then, the Board should ask outside experts to prepare special briefings such as the *Strategy Execution Audit*™, that address the salient points raised by the questions.

Finally, the comments that accompany the questions in this monograph are intended to provide Directors with a framework for critically assessing the answers they are given and for digging deeper if necessary. The comments summarize current thinking on the issues and the practices of leading corporations.

Introduction:
Corporate Directors and
Strategy Execution

This is the first publication in the world to provide guidance to Boards on their responsibility for strategy execution. While there have been documents detailing the role of the Board in developing, reviewing and approving strategy[1] to date, there has been no direction given to Boards on how they can and should enhance their organization's ability to execute the strategy.

But, why should the Board concern itself with strategy execution?

Research continues to confirm that when it comes to identifying the sources of organizational failures, only 10% of companies fall short of their goals and objectives from having formulated a poor strategy in the first place. Meanwhile, 90% fail due to poor-to-lousy execution of an otherwise good strategic plan. As a result, considerable value is left on the table and never realized.

---

1   *20 Questions the Board Should Ask About Strategy* by Chris Bart, Ph.D., FCPA, 2012

This research is backed up by experience and publicly stated reflections of highly admired corporate leaders. Lou Gerstner, former Chairman and CEO of IBM has stated repeatedly that: "Success is 5% strategy and 95% execution," Larry Bossidy, former AlliedSignal CEO has declared: "Strategies most often fail because they aren't well executed." And Scott Adams, the creator of the famous comic strip *Dilbert*, said it perhaps even more succinctly:

"Ideas are worthless. Execution is everything."

So, while there seems to be wide acknowledgement of the importance of strategy execution, the reality is that corporate Directors continue to focus most of their energy on making sure their organization has developed the right strategy and give very little attention to the **_organizational arrangements_** required for its successful execution. Perhaps their prior education may have a lot to do with this. After all, the vast majority of courses on *strategy* taught at the undergraduate, MBA and executive education levels focus primarily — or even exclusively — on strategy formulation; i.e., the process of matching perceived market opportunities with an organization's available resources.

In contrast, there are only a scant number of programs offering insight and advice on *strategy execution,* which involves *the art of focusing organizational effort (activities and behaviors) to make the strategy a reality.* The corporate emphasis on strategy development is compounded further when one considers the fact that some of the world's very best strategy-consulting firms are known for simply walking away from their clients after helping them identify or develop a strategy.

With all the emphasis on having the right strategy, it should come as no surprise that when companies experience "an execution gap"— the shortfall between the expected strategic outcomes and their actual performance — they prefer to blame the strategy instead of finding and fixing the more likely *root cause* problems in execution. As a result, executives are furiously fired or the organization is routinely reorganized and reorganized and reorganized. Yet, the execution gap persists. That's because an execution gap is usually not related to a single individual or business or functional unit — although it can be.

Rather, execution gaps are most often the result of *commitment and culture issues* which in turn are due to the misalignment of a company's currently existing organizational arrangements (i.e., systems, processes, procedures, polices and projects) and its intended strategy. In fact, it is a truism that every company is perfectly aligned "organizationally" to focus its members' activities and *behaviors* in some fashion to produce its current results. Accordingly, if a Board and its management want to change performance outcomes, they need to change their company's organizational arrangements because the current alignment—or rather misalignment—is what's stopping the company from executing its strategy to achieve the results desired.

In our own research and experience, we have confirmed the opinion of Jamie Dimon, CEO of JPMorgan Chase, who said: "I'd rather have a first-rate execution and second-rate strategy any time than a brilliant idea and mediocre management." In other words, a solid "B-level" strategy that is executed well will beat an "A-level" strategy executed poorly. A lot of money is being spent each year by companies seeking an "A-level" strategy. However reality suggests in fact, that creating one is really not that difficult. It's making the strategy a reality that's the problem! And, the source of that problem is the existence of one or more execution gaps. Accordingly, we have come to believe that Boards should not only assume oversight responsibility for the quality of their firm's corporate strategy, but also for its successful execution.

The following set of 20 Essential Questions represents *the world's first complete and comprehensive governance framework* to help corporate Directors fulfill their responsibilities for overseeing the execution of their organization's strategy. They are designed to help Boards and their managements tackle the execution gaps that are holding back performance and to give their organization what we like to call the Execution Edge™.

While the questions we pose are presented in a particular order, individual Directors may prefer to begin at different points in the framework. *It is strongly recommended, though, that Directors consider all of the questions.*

"Facts do not cease to exist because they are ignored."

— Aldous Huxley

 WARNING:

Some of these questions might seem to be beyond the traditional scope of a Board's responsibility and non-progressive Directors will attempt to use the old "micromanagement argument" both to avoid asking them and to shout down those directors who want the questions answered. While Boards should respect the division of responsibility between themselves and management, in today's environment of greater stakeholder scrutiny of corporate performance, these questions provide new guidance to Directors on one of their most important responsibilities that has been traditionally neglected i.e., *making sure the organization is capable of executing its strategy and providing ongoing oversight to it.*

Directors can no longer simply wash their hands once the strategy has been reviewed and approved by the Board and then blithely blame management when execution fails. All the evidence to date suggests failure is likely to happen if the Board is not giving proper attention to the execution of their organization's strategy. Indeed, given the magnitude of the problem, we predict that the board's oversight responsibility for strategy execution will become the "next wave in corporate governance."

The 20 Essential Questions

Strategy

Strategy defines the "relationship" which an organization seeks
to have with its environment and stakeholders.

— Chris Bart, FCPA

Question 1

Is the organization executing against the right strategy? Or put another way: Have management and the Board established an "excellent strategy" for the organization to pursue?

Notwithstanding the fact that no organization should attempt to execute its strategy unless it is convinced and has confirmed that the strategy is an excellent one, the track record of firms attempting to implement inadequate, or downright bad and misguided strategies is frightening. The corporate graveyard is littered with the corpses of once great companies that set themselves on a course to execute disastrous strategies.

As a reality check, Boards and their managements need to thoughtfully and critically assure themselves that the strategy successfully passes the two essential tests that define truly great strategies:

> **TEST 1:** Has the strategy identified a well-researched market opportunity that will enable the organization to achieve its financial objectives while meeting customer expectations better than those it competes against?

> **TEST 2:** Does the organization have the internal resources already on hand — or quickly obtainable — which will allow the organization to pursue and capture the opportunity?

If the answer to either of these questions is "no", then the strategy has failed to meet the essential conditions required prior to execution. The Board, therefore, should send management back to the drawing board until both conditions are met.

Even when both conditions appear to be met, Boards and their managements should consider giving themselves a period of reflection (i.e., a cooling off period), preferably one to two weeks after the euphoria of having approved the final version of the strategic plan has subsided. They should do this to assure themselves *one final time* that the strategy really meets the two tests of strategic greatness. [2]

> *"A strategy, even a great one,*
> *doesn't implement itself."*
>
> — Anonymous

---

2   For a more fulsome discussion on the role of the board in setting the strategic direction of an organization, readers are encouraged review the publication: *20 Essential Questions Corporate Directors Should Ask About Strategy* by Dr. Chris Bart, FCPA, 2012.

Communication and Awareness

"Strategy communication: when you are tired of telling the strategy story, you have probably reached 3% of the target population."

— Anonymous

Question 2

Is the strategy known *and* remembered by all members of the organization—from the C-suite to the front line?

For a strategy to be successfully executed, it must be *the primary focus of the entire organization. Accordingly, the first step in this focusing process is that the organization's strategy be clearly and unambiguously communicated from the C-suite to the front line.* Boards, however, cannot and should not take it for granted that everyone has been "told" about the strategy in some fashion. In fact, many Boards continue to believe naively that putting out an internal memo or a video means that everyone has even heard the strategic message. Thus, a Board — as part of its oversight of strategic execution — should seek to gain reasonable assurance not only that everyone has been "told" the strategic message but also that it was both "received" and is being remembered.

A simple and highly effective "test" for this is that everyone must be able to articulate the strategy completely or at least recite its salient priorities. Again, the reason for this is to have *complete alignment* among all employees, including the Board, in terms of what the organization is attempting to achieve through execution.

Sadly, this seldom happens and there are three primary reasons for this:

Reason A: the CEO has not *sufficiently communicated* with his executives and so the C-suite itself is not unambiguously aligned with the strategy! As a result, when individuals under each C-suite executive meet and compare notes, they quickly discover that they have received conflicting and inconsistent messages from the top. Now the question is: who to believe? Failure to address this can cause paralysis among middle managers

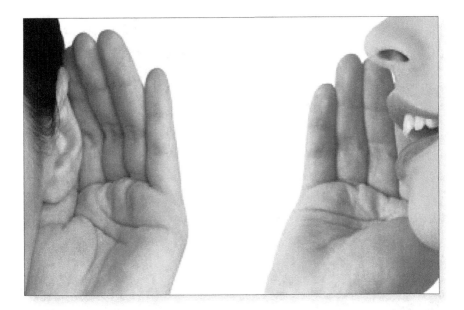

with each one individually afraid they might be going down the wrong path. When this happens, everyone freezes and execution stops dead in its tracks.

Reason B: Even with C-suite alignment, when strategic messages are "cascaded" from senior to junior managers and then to the front line, it is almost guaranteed that they will not be "transmitted and translated" consistently — just like a favorite birthday game that children play called "whisper down the lane", or "children's telephone". One child *whispers* a message into the ear of a child sitting beside him/her (e.g., "Harry likes to play baseball in the summer"), who then does the same to the child on the other side, and so on. When the last child hears the message, he/she is asked to repeat it out loud to the whole group, e.g., "Mary hikes every day and says it's a bummer."

Ironically, many big companies do exactly the same thing thinking that they are supposedly "cascading" the strategy, with the CEO communicating to his/her direct reports who then tell their employees, and so on.

Just like the children's game, the final communication of the strategy will be vastly different from the original and the company runs the risk of ending up with multiple strategies being executed at the front line instead of just one.

Reason C: The primary enemy of having a strategy "heard" and "remembered" is the din or cacophony of messages competing for share-of-mind attention. Psychologists estimate that the average individual is sent seventeen thousand "messages" a day. So the probability of any one message registering and consistently "sticking" is fairly low. What to do? The legendary CEO of GE, Jack Welch, noted that when he got to GE, he was confusing employees with *too many messages, infrequently communicated.* So, he boiled them down to 2-3 key "thoughts" that he and his senior executives *repeated relentlessly.* And so it goes: simplicity and repetition are important instruments for muscling important strategic messages into the consciousness of employees.

The bottom line: Directors must ensure that there is real alignment within both the Board itself and the C-suite on the strategy. They should also look for assurance from their CEOs that they accept responsibility for the accurate communication of the key "strategy messages" to be communicated down the line.

One way of doing this is to make sure there is a comprehensive strategy communication and engagement action plan in place to help every employee begin connecting with the strategy.

N.B.: If a Board and its management fail in the communication of the strategy, the execution will be undermined by its own leadership!! To quote Pogo:

Question 3

Has management established appropriate metrics to define and specify the successful execution of the strategy?

Metrics are the first *essential stage* for helping Boards and their managements to translate, measure and judge the progress being made in executing their strategy. Metrics help convert the strategy and its salient components (i.e., the mission, vision and values) into specific performance targets/objectives and thus create yardsticks for tracking organizational performance. Metrics may be quantitative or qualitative in nature. The key is that they are measurable.

Often, the metrics upon which most organizations like to focus are *financial outcome measures* with the most popular being an organization's profitability. In the case of publicly traded companies, profitability is usually expressed in terms of their 'market value' or 'earnings per share'. However, while important, profitability should not be seen as either the most significant or only objective to emphasize. This is because current profitability has been shown to be a poor predictor for future performance. Moreover, notwithstanding the effects of business cycles and market disruptions, CEOs and their CFOs have many ways in which to impact an organization's current profitability to the detriment of its longer-term sustainability. Boards thus need to gain assurance that the future of their company is not being compromised by the present actions of its management.

The way for them to gain such assurance is to make sure that there are a set of strategic metrics *that:*

- Are appropriate to the strategy's direction and aspirations

- Reflect the sources of the organization's current _and future_ profitability and competitiveness, and

- Assure the Board that management is considering the interests of all key stakeholders whose support is needed to achieve the strategy

Typical examples of *strategic metrics* would include: market share, customer satisfaction and loyalty, employee engagement, cost leadership, technological superiority, environmental and social responsibility etc. See Exhibit 1 for an example of how selected financial and strategic metrics might be aligned with an organization's strategy and shape its execution.

EXHIBIT 1

STRATEGY	METRICS
Growth	Return on Investment Number of New Products Strategic Drivers • Customer Service • Product Quality • Technical Leadership Market Share (increase)
Profitability	Return on Investment Cash Flow Strategic Drivers • Customer Satisfaction • Employee Engagement • Cost Leadership Market Share (maintenance)

Question 4

Is it clear to each person in the organization – from the C-suite to the front line – what specific actions and *behaviors* are required from them both individually and collectively to execute the strategy flawlessly?

The great philosopher Humpty Dumpty once said: "When I use a word, it means just what I choose it to mean — neither more nor less."3 Thus, the communication required and described in Question 2 does not assure *understanding*. Boards need assurance that everyone in the organization knows the strategy, but also, more importantly, what they are expected to do, individually and collectively, about it. It is this "personalized understanding" that moves strategy to the specifics of execution.

For whatever reasons, however, too many Boards and their managements delude themselves into thinking that everyone is *behaviorally aligned* around the strategy and that the tasks and actions of every individual can somehow be linked to — and justified by — the strategy. But this is seldom the case. In fact, most employees – but especially those at the front line where "strategy meets reality" – confess that they do not clearly understand what their company's strategy means for them in their particular jobs or what exactly they are expected to be doing to make a contribution to its execution?4 Yet, this is not that surprising when, according

---

3   *Through the Looking Glass* by Lewis Carroll
4   In the 2012 best selling book, *A Tale of Two Employees and the Person Who Wanted to Lead Them* (by Chris Bart, FCPA), it shows vividly what happens when employees do not understand the company's strategy and mission. Moreover, research from the Copenhagen School of Business found that when employees do not know the company's strategy or mission they could not care less because they did not understand how they were involved in its execution.

to an American study, it was reported that less than 50 percent of C-suite executives surveyed could effectively articulate their own individual priorities emanating from the current strategy.

In contrast, the most successful companies assure that every employee clearly understands both what is expected of them in terms of performance outcomes and the specific project inputs, activities and behaviors required from them to make those outcomes happen. And they regularly test for this by routinely asking employees in meetings, in hallways, etc. what the organization's strategy is but also *what their individual role is in contributing to its achievement.*

Accordingly, once their CEO's strategic message has been sent, Boards must follow-up to gain reasonable assurance that it is also *unambiguously understood* by all employees as it moves down the line and that each person knows exactly and specifically how to execute their jobs against it. This translation of strategy from the C-suite to the front line is illustrated diagrammatically in Figure 1 below.

Figure 1   **Delivering Strategy to the Front Line**

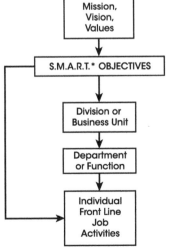

*S.M.A.R.T. objectives are those which are
specific, measurable, acceptable, realistic and timely

Integration

"Strategy without tactics is the slowest route to victory. Tactics without strategy is the noise before defeat."

—Sun Tzu

Question 5

Does management have a reasonable action plan to inform and engage the company's "external partners" in the strategy and what is expected of them in terms of its execution?

Every company has external business partners. These may be vendors, distributors, retailers, suppliers, advertising and PR agencies, or brokers. Many companies have also outsourced their manufacturing, call center and distribution operations both to cut costs, and to focus on their core competencies. While these business arrangements may make good business sense, they can, if not properly managed undermine execution of the company's overall strategy and have unintended consequences.

For example, toy manufacturer Mattel* once made the decision to outsource the manufacturing of its products to China in an effort to cut costs. Later, it was discovered that lead-based paint — a major cause of liver and brain injury in young children—was being used in the production of its toys. To deflect criticism, Mattel's CEO blamed the Chinese plants for not following Mattel's strict production guidelines. Unfortunately for Mattel, an enquiry revealed that the Chinese plants had not actually been given the guidelines about Mattel's health policies or to not use lead paint. The Chinese plants were only given instructions to make the toys inexpensively. Eventually, Mattel's CEO had to fly to China and appear on Chinese national television to publicly apologize for blaming its Chinese partners. The incident also hurt Mattel's Christmas sales since parents were wary of buying *any* of their toys.

Additionally, more than ever before, companies are being held increasingly responsible for the execution errors of their partners — no matter how distantly "related" those partners may be. For instance, while WalMart did not select the Bangladesh plant used to manufacture some of its products, its reputation was damaged and it may be legally responsible for failing to enforce its own safety standards on the facility when a horrific fire broke out killing more than one hundred workers. [5]

But it's not just outsourced manufacturing that can cause execution problems. They can come from any "partner" in the supply chain. For instance, outsourced sales and marketing communications programs that are not both tightly linked to the overall corporate strategy and well integrated with other internal activities (see also Question 6) can quickly take a company "off message" with customers and also undermine strategy execution with employees.

AEP, a large utility company based in Columbus, Ohio, serves as a good example of this issue. At one point in its history, the company's ad agency proposed that a major media campaign touting AEP's financial support of Cirque du Soleil would help its "CSR" (Corporate Social Responsibility) activities and uniquely differentiate the company with investors, regulators and its communities. Simultaneously, AEP's internal communications informed employees that any salary increases would be "modest" because the company was seeking to save money.

Upon seeing their company's advertisements supporting the Cirque, employees became upset. They could not understand what the company's backing of the Cirque had to do with a utility and how this was a wise use of the company's resources. The employee complaints eventually caught the attention of both the local media and public officials. Instead of be-

---

5   "Bangladesh Fire: What WalMart's Supplier Network Missed," *The Wall Street Journal* http://on.wsj.com/T2xoC1

ing praised, the company was ridiculed and chastised for its "unwise" and "costly" decisions. Some even inquired why a regional utility would fund a group of performers with no ties to the local community. Employees especially started questioning their supervisors and wondered aloud why only modest salary increases could be expected when the company had money to splurge for "circuses."

As these examples vividly demonstrate, no matter where a company's external partners are in its supply chain, it is vitally important that they know — just as the internal ones do — the company's strategy and understand what is expected of them in terms of their contribution to its successful execution. Accordingly, Directors should look for evidence that adequate procedures are in place for the proper supervision of major activities undertaken by external partners and that those activities are being implemented in line with the corporate strategy.

Question 6

Are all of the operating plans in the company integrated so that they build from the same strategy?

While Boards are supposed to actively engage with management in establishing the organization's strategy, they are expected only to provide high-level *oversight* when it comes to management's running of the company on a day-to-day basis[6]. Consequently, it is management who takes responsibility for the development and content of the detailed operating plan which puts "flesh and bones" on a corporation's strategy. Typically, the operating plan addresses all of the major functional areas, such as marketing and sales, finance, human resources, manufacturing, information technology, etc. As such, it involves a myriad of specific details and action plans (typically referred to as *tactics*) concerning the way management intends to achieve the strategy.

It is essential, however, that the various portions of the operating plan concerning the functional units be both individually linked to the strategy and tightly connected with one another. Otherwise, execution of the overall strategy will be compromised.

While Boards are generally encouraged to refrain from assessing and approving the details of the organization's operating plans, knowing that this integration in the operating plan exists should still be a major concern for Boards. The corporation's overall strategy should lead and inform all other sub-unit plans and there should be clear evidence that the business unit and functional strategies have been tied to it.

---

6   For a more detailed discussion of the highly circumscribed role of the board in providing oversight to the operating plan, see Question 9 in *20 Essential Questions Corporate Directors Should Ask About Strategy,* by Dr. Chris Bart, FCPA, 2012.

Unfortunately, in too many companies, the corporate strategy is a "roll up exercise" of the functional and business unit strategies. When this occurs, the organization runs the risk of the end product strategy becoming a case of "the tail wagging the dog." A company, however, cannot simply be a compilation of its sub-unit strategies. There must be some overarching and overriding focus that dominates, dictates and links together the activities of the various parts. Boards, therefore, should ask questions to gain reasonable assurance that their organization's operating plan is sufficiently integrated and aligned with the corporate strategy. And they should demand evidence that this integration exists.

Culture and Risk

"We're a company with $70 billion in revenues.
But we could be a $90 billion company
if only we could execute better."

— Chairman & CEO,
Fortune 500 Company

Question 7
Does the organization's culture support the strategy's execution?

There's often a mistaken belief that strategy and cultural values are separate. However, as management guru Peter Drucker famously noted "Culture eats strategy for breakfast." This is because culture governs the way employees feel, think and act. As such it can, and usually does, have a more powerful effect on human motivation than strategy. In fact, a strategy will mean nothing—and go nowhere—if the organizational culture is not appropriate to support it.

For instance, consider the organizational values required to successfully integrate the operating plans referred to in Question 6. According to a survey conducted by the Center for Creative Leadership, 97% of leaders at the senior executive level, 91% at the middle management level, and 43% at the entry-level cited *collaboration and cooperation across organizational boundaries* as important cultural values for organizational sustainability and achieving a competitive advantage However, only 53% of senior executives, 19% of middle managers and just 8% of entry level managers claimed that this was actually happening within their respective peer groups.[7]

Clearly, the existence of "silos" is a serious organizational phenomenon deleterious to strategic execution. But simply expecting individuals to join forces for the common good does not appear to be something that is going to happen naturally. In fact, self-interest has been shown to generate competition more than cooperation.

---

7   "Boundary Spanning Leadership", Center for Creative Leadership, Jeffrey Yip, Chris Ernst, and Michael Campbell, Center for Creative Leadership, 2011.

Culture, however, starts at the top and Boards must "own" it jointly with their senior management team. They should not abdicate this responsibility and attempt to delegate stewardship of the organization's values solely to the CEO. A Board therefore, needs to assess the cultural values of its organization and determine to what extent the values support the strategy and its execution. Values include the norms, beliefs and *behaviors* that define the way employees are expected to interact with one another.

Where the values are found lacking, the C-suite must be given clear direction by the Board on what cultural values it is expected to embrace and demonstrate on a daily basis (e.g., collaboration, honesty, passion, persuasion (not command & control), etc.) both in service of the strategy's execution and as leadership examples for aspiring, lower level managers. These expected behaviors may also need to be incorporated into the organization's accountability system (see Question 12 on page 35).

Question 8

Have all the principal risks that could threaten successful execution of the strategy (and its related activities) been identified? Are they being routinely monitored? And are mechanisms in place to deal with them should they materialize?

Risk is defined as the "effect of uncertainty on objectives."[8] As such, all strategies involve risk, and all risk involves uncertainty. It is also an accepted truism that risk and reward often go hand in hand. Consequently, where an intended strategy promises very high returns relative to existing market conditions, there will invariably also be very high risks attached to it. The converse is also true: low risk, low rewards. Understandably, then, one of the greatest fears for both Boards and management is that they may not have identified a major risk that, if it materializes, could undermine the execution of the strategy or which, if known earlier on, would have deterred them from pursuing the strategy in the first place.

Some research suggests that this fear is well justified. A study by McKinsey & Company found that only 60% of Directors claimed to understand their company's risks. The more disturbing finding, however, was that a staggering 82% of managers believed that their Directors did not understand those risks. Since the Board has ultimate responsibility for setting the risk appetite of the company, McKinsey's findings should concern Directors. They suggest that either Directors think they understand more about their organization's risks than they actually do, or worse, that management is not being completely forthcoming with them regarding all of the risks facing the company... or both.

---

8   ISO 31000 (2009) Risk management — Principles and guidelines

While risks have typically been categorized as being financial or operational, the greatest source of organizational failures has come from strategic risks: the risk that the strategy chosen was the wrong one (i.e., usually because of low demand or overwhelming competition) and/or the inability of the company to successfully execute it (usually due to inferior or unattainable resources or organizational/cultural misalignment). In fact, according to Corporate Executive Board (CEB), 68% of *risk events* are strategic in nature and responsible for destroying more than 50% of firms' market capitalization.[9] The CEB report also estimated that auditors spend about 80% of their time providing assurance on traditional areas such as financial and compliance risks, even though these risks make up only 18% of the drivers of financial decline.

Directors therefore need to have confidence that adequate processes designed to identify, mitigate and monitor strategic risks are in place.[10] One underutilized way of doing this is to demand that strategic risk be part of the internal audit activities of the company. This audit should include not only the risks from having a bad corporate strategy, but also the risks occurring from poor alignment of the organization's structure, systems, processes and policies with a good strategy.

---

9   http://www.businessweek.com/managing/content/jul2010/ca2010072_086225.htm

10   For more information on the methodology for enterprise risk management, see *Enterprise Risk Management – Today's Leading Research and Best Practices for Tomorrow's Executives* by J. Fraser. and B.J. Simkins (Editors), Wiley, 2010.

Capability

"When planning for a year, plant corn.
When planning for a decade, plant trees.
When planning for life, train and educate people."

— Chinese Proverb

Question 9

Is the organization's hiring/recruitment system aligned with the strategy? Are individuals being hired for positions and/or relocated within the organization based primarily on their ability to contribute to the execution of the strategy?

With their Board's constructive input, most CEOs are capable of developing a very good strategy. Yet, it has been reported that over 70% of CEO terminations and "early retirements" have been due to their inability to execute that strategy.[11] Clearly, successful strategy execution begins with having the right CEO in place to turn the approved strategy into reality. Also, the days of having a "universal CEO" who can lead and manage any organization are over. In a world of increasing specialization, Boards need to spend more time thinking about the kinds of specialist execution skills and cultural orientation required in their CEOs that need to be aligned with the strategy. One example of this CEO-strategy alignment is shown in Exhibit 2.

Additionally, while the Board has, by tradition, restricted its responsibility for hiring and firing to the CEO's position only, there are now more calls for Boards to expand their oversight of the C-suite and in particular those "officers" of the corporation who play a vital role in the strategy's execution. And with good reason. In many companies, there are C-suite executives who either don't understand the strategy, do not care about the strategy, or who actually undermine the strategy for their own personal objectives. One notable and recent example is Steven Sinofsky, former head of Microsoft's Windows division, who suddenly "resigned."

---

11 http://money.cnn.com/magazines/fortune/fortune_archive/1999/06/21/261696/index.htm

Sinofsky was known for his brilliance, but perhaps even more for his abrasiveness and arrogance. According to a number of sources, he was a potential successor to CEO Steve Balmer. There were also too many stories of Sinofsky's unwillingness to "play nice with others" – and this was allowed to persist, some say for much too long. It took a lot of effort for Balmer to remove Sinofsky, especially since his success had gained him supporters among both employees and the Board.

Problems in the selection of C-suite executives are further revealed in one national study, in which CEOs were asked the extent to which they would re-hire their existing management team. Astonishingly, 36% responded that they would rehire less than 50%! With these kinds of *hiring errors* obviously being made, Boards need to start probing deeper and asking whether its most senior executives below the CEO fit the desired culture of the company and if they truly understand and are committed to the strategy. To the extent that any doubts emerge, strategic execution could be compromised.

EXHIBIT 2

DIFFERENT STRATEGIES REQUIRE DIFFERENT MANAGERS

	STRATEGY	
	Growth	**Cash Flow**
Managerial Alignment Requirements	Visionary Innovator/entrepreneurial Not afraid of taking risks Focus is on the future Deferred profitability Seeks/accepts change Team oriented	Practical realist Efficiency-seeking Avoids risk Focus is here-and-now Current results Avoids/dislikes change Individualist

Question 10

To the extent that individual skills and/or competencies required to execute the strategy are missing, is the organization's training system aligned to close this execution gap?

To execute a strategy, everyone in the organization must be both willing and able to do the tasks that they have been assigned. If employees are able but not willing, the organization has a personnel motivation issue. On the other hand, if employees are willing, but not able, the organization has a training issue. Both willingness and ability are required for strategy execution and it is important to understand why there are gaps in employee performance even when they are experienced.

Many organizations, however, fail to properly assess whether they have a willingness problem or an ability issue. Interestingly, more often than not, the issue is training. Yet many organizations hastily and incorrectly assume that employees are unwilling to cooperate or to do what is needed to execute the strategy. Regrettably, this leads to many unnecessary reorganizations and firings.

In one major company with some of the worst customer satisfaction numbers in its industry, the assumption at first was that the organization had a problem hiring good people. Upon further investigation, it was determined that the major cause of the problems was a capability issue: its *customer-facing employees* did not have proper training in handling and rectifying customer complaints. In fact, to boost profits executives cut customer service activities and budgets that included hiring and training qualified people.

Employees soon got the message that despite the company's mission statement exhorting them to "delight customers," management did not value customer service. A first-class CRM (Customer Relations Management) training program was subsequently installed to fix the problem and to bring the much needed customer service skills into alignment with the strategy. The training translated into significantly improved customer satisfaction numbers and a reduction in customer defections.

Directors therefore need to ask about the training and development implications of the approved strategy, how any training requirements have been incorporated and budgeted into the HR plan and what the time lag is between the training and seeing its actual benefits through execution. There should also be some indication in the operational plans that improvements will not be seen until the required training has taken place.

Acountability and Recognition

"However beautiful the strategy,
you should occasionally look at the results."

—Sir Winston Churchill

Question 11

Are the company's IT systems designed to meet the organization's strategy execution objectives?

It wasn't that long ago that information technology (IT) systems were of little concern to Boards. However, Directors globally have been expressing a growing concern about both their company's IT systems, especially the costs and risks they represent, and the general lack of "IT literacy" that most Directors have about technology.

Indeed, business operations have become increasingly reliant on IT, and with the convergence of the business and IT environments comes new kinds of opportunities, but also vulnerabilities, risks, and threats. As proof, more and more companies appear to be having IT security issues, particularly with respect to IT integration failures post-M&A, and systems problems (e.g., "overloads") that have caused customer relations issues. These are all legitimate Board concerns because they undermine the value of the firm.

As with all organizational systems, when a strategic decision is made, the Board should enquire into how the organization's IT systems will be used or modified to facilitate and support the execution of the strategy. Directors should be particularly interested in raising questions about how well IT is integrated with risk management. The Board's audit and risk committees also need assurance that their organization has a coordinated governance, risk and compliance management approach. As noted throughout this book, too often functional units such as IT become siloed from the organization's strategy and that, in turn, is a recipe for execution problems.

Question 12

Has accountability been established for the execution and ultimate achievement of the strategy?

As part of its organizational arrangements to establish accountability for a strategy's successful execution, it is extremely important that the system for evaluating individual and team performance *aligns precisely* with the strategy. All employees, from the C-suite to the lowest level, must be "encouraged" to *continuously commit and submit* to make the specific outcomes that shape and define each strategy's uniqueness a reality. Sometimes, that commitment is easily won once a person simply knows what to do and how.

More often, though, that's simply not enough. This is where there needs to be an *accountability system* that tightly couples — "aligns" — *the specific results expected from a particular strategy with actual performance.* Otherwise, an organization can find itself in the position of rewarding for "strategy B" while expecting to achieve "strategy A." An example of this alignment for two different types of strategies is provided in Exhibit 3. The exhibit illustrates especially the distinctiveness with which *similar* performance evaluation criteria can be highly aligned and fine-tuned for their specific strategies.

Boards therefore need to consider the extent to which the performance evaluation criteria of the CEO and senior management team capture both the macro and *nuanced* elements of their strategy's aspirations, and to take action when they do not. In one large global organization, the Board noted that despite the acknowledged strategic goal of increased cross-selling among four divisions, little activity had occurred on this front. When questioned on this, the CEO and each executive provided explanations as to why this was *"really not possible"* given their other priorities. The Board, however, believed that this was an essential component of the strategy's success and subsequently insisted that their performance evaluation criteria make cross-selling a major part of their executive compensation bonus.

Miraculously, cross-selling began to flourish, thus reinforcing the notion that it is not only the type of performance evaluation criteria that must be aligned with a strategy but *also the degree to which the various criteria are emphasized -- and rewarded (see Questions 13 and 14 below).*

Exhibit 3

Aligning Executive Evaluation Criteria with the Strategy

STRATEGY	METRICS	WEIGHT
Growth	Return on Investment	15%
	Cash flow	0%
	Strategic drivers:	
	• customer service	15%
	• product quality	15%
	• technical leadership	15%
	Market share (increase)	40%
		100%
Profitability	Return on Investment	25%
	Cash flow	20%
	Strategic drivers:	
	• customer satisfaction	20%
	• employee engagement	10%
	• cost leadership	10%
	Market share (maintenance)	15%
		100%

Question 13

Is the performance evaluation "review process" aligned with the strategy's execution?

As stated above in Question 12, it is important that an organization's performance evaluation system be aligned with the strategy. But not just any performance evaluation *review process* will do. The goal of a performance review should primarily be to help an employee enhance performance in the future and improve the strategy's execution. Yet, according to most CEOs, their evaluations are often both too late and unhelpful in terms of corrective action.

It is therefore recommended that Boards switch gears and carry out a *review process designed to **enhance** the performance of their CEO*, not the typical one that primarily seeks to criticize and find fault with his or her performance. The CEO especially should not be learning only at the time of the formal year-end review how he or she has done during the past year.

Instead, good Boards review an organization's strategy execution performance continuously and pass this information on to their executives along with their thoughts on how *execution gaps* might be corrected and closed. Performance reviews designed to enhance performance, of course, require Directors with the skills, competencies, experience and time to conduct them. To the extent that they are not able to give these types of review, Boards and their governance committees need to reflect on the skill sets of individuals that are being nominated onto the Board.

Performance enhancing reviews, however, also need to be completed for employees down the line. Accordingly, to enhance strategic execution, Boards should seek confirmation that such reviews are being conducted throughout the entire organization. They should ask, in particular, to see any 360-degree evaluations of all key executives of the company—but certainly of all corporate officers. They also need to determine to what degree support staff (finance, human resources, internal audit, legal, investor relations, etc.) are focusing on supporting the business units and functions in furtherance of their strategy execution efforts, as opposed to just "auditing them for compliance" or adopting a "nothing's changed" attitude. Indeed, in a world where uncertainty and massive change is a daily occurrence, any comment from an oversight function that says "nothing is changed" should be regarded as a "red light" that the oversight function is not working properly.

Question 14

Are the right types of rewards and incentives aligned with the strategy?

It is a tenet of human psychology that individuals will do the things they are *rewarded* — or *"incentivized"* — to do. Fortunately, organizations have a variety of rewards and incentives, formal and informal, monetary and non-monetary, with which to motivate individuals in their quest to successfully execute the strategy. An important question for Boards to ask, however, is whether or not the organization has chosen the right incentives given the nature of the strategy.

As Exhibit 4 illustrates, not all incentives are created equal and some rewards—as with the case of performance evaluation criteria—may be more appropriate for the execution of certain types of strategies than others. It is strongly recommended, therefore that Boards seek the services of executive compensation professionals to help ensure that an appropriate set of incentives has been selected to match the strategy's direction and inherent risks.

Exhibit 4

ALIGNING COMPENSATION WITH STRATEGY

"Growth" Strategy Manager	"Profitability" Strategy Manager
Benefits & Perquisites $150,000	Benefits $100,000
Capital Stock $400,000	Cash Bonus $200,000
Cash Bonus $400,000	Salary $700,000
Salary $400,000	
Total Package $1,350,000	Total Package $1,000,000

Sometimes, though there is no amount of "encouragement" that will change a person who is unwilling to "play well with others". Accordingly, there must be known penalties ("negative rewards") for those who refuse to align their *behaviors* and actions with the strategy. Since most organizations fail due to poor execution, Boards need to embrace the notion that when it comes to their strategic responsibilities, "Execution is Everything™", and the incentive compensation system is the ultimate expression of the seriousness with which an organization and its Board believe this!

Boards therefore need to seek assurance that their organization's incentives are aligned *at multiple levels* with the strategy. Equally important, they need to make sure that those individuals, functions and business units who have executed their portions of the strategy well are rewarded and recognized *even if the overall firm has a bad year*!

Board Specific
Execution Activities

"With great power comes great responsibility."

— Stan Lee, Marvel Comics.

Question 15

How is the Board demonstrating to the CEO and other members of senior management *on an ongoing basis* that they are concerned about strategy execution?

Once the strategy has been approved, urgent matters will invariably materialize whereby a Board and its management inadvertently can get distracted in their quest to stay focused on executing the organization's strategy. To avoid this from happening, it is important that the Board regularly and routinely communicates to the CEO, clearly and unambiguously, about the importance of strategy execution and holds management accountable for delivering the agreed upon strategy and its performance metrics.

At a minimum, a portion of the agenda of every Board meeting should be devoted to a discussion of the progress that the organization is making in terms of executing the strategy. This discussion should include the identification of any currently discovered — or emerging — *execution gaps* as well as management's plans for addressing them. The Board must not shy away from offering its management any performance enhancing "suggestions" while being mindful of the need *to not cross the line* and micromanage the CEO.

Question 16

If the Board is to sign off on the corporate strategy, what should it do to assure itself that the strategy will be executed properly?

Obviously, it is always prudent to close the proverbial barn door before the horses escape. Given the research findings that only 10% of companies successfully execute their strategy, most Boards — unless they have sufficient evidence to the contrary — can safely assume that they are amongst the 90% of companies that will experience difficulties in execution. A good Board therefore worries about the organization's ability to execute the strategy before giving final approval to it. One easy way of doing this is to utilize the questions in this document to probe the CEO and other senior managers to determine the extent to which the entire company will be passionately committed to delivering the strategy.

An even faster way for the Board to find out if and where there are execution problems is to do a *Strategy Execution Audit*™. This audit can help the Board determine the degree to which the C-suite and Board are aligned with the strategy and whether the top executives understand what exactly they are executing against. After all, if the senior team is not aligned, the organization cannot be.

Additionally, the audit tests for the alignment of organizational resources and assesses whether or not only those projects and initiatives that contribute to the strategy's realization get funded. It also gauges the degree to which the organizational structures, systems, policies and procedures found in the functional and business units are being used to effectively coordinate, control and focus employee activities and *behaviors* in accordance with the strategy.

This organizational alignment framework is illustrated diagrammatically in Figure 2. Finally, the *Strategy Execution Audit™* determines if any outside "partners" (e.g., supply chain partners, advertising, legal and PR firms, as well as others) are executing appropriately on the strategy.

Figure 2

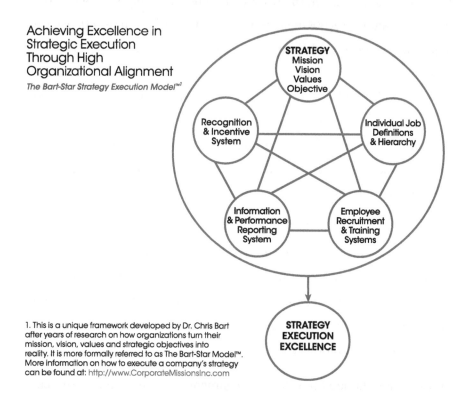

Achieving Excellence in
Strategic Execution
Through High
Organizational Alignment
The Bart-Star Strategy Execution Model™[1]

1. This is a unique framework developed by Dr. Chris Bart after years of research on how organizations turn their mission, vision, values and strategic objectives into reality. It is more formally referred to as The Bart-Star Model™. More information on how to execute a company's strategy can be found at: http://www.CorporateMissionsInc.com

The result of the *Strategy Execution Audit™* is the identification of both major and minor execution gaps as well as the fixes to close them and thereby enhance *Execution Excellence™*.

But even if a Board believes that they are one of the lucky 10% of outstanding companies that successfully avoids errors in execution, it is worthwhile to consider having a *Strategy Execution Audit*™, if only to confirm that there are no *execution gaps* and that the company is aligned and executing to the fullest extent possible.

A more detailed description of the *Strategy Execution Audit*™ is contained in Appendix 1.

Question 17

What will management do with the information from the *Strategy Execution Audit*™ to demonstrate to the Board and ensure that execution gaps™ are closed?

Organizations are systems. Accordingly, execution problems and their organizational impact are seldom restricted to one area of a company. Execution problems that are identified as originating in one part of an organization often create execution problems for one or more other parts. Because of this, developing the solution(s) to close an execution gap typically requires the input of all those affected by its existence.

Just as developing a great strategy calls for the contribution and input of individuals and units throughout the organization, the same holds true in terms of solving execution problems. Indeed, experience has shown that when companies work out their execution problems as a team, they capture the elusive *"Execution Edge*™*"* that helps catapult them more efficiently and effectively in their execution efforts. The fastest and best way to break down any organizational silos that may impede solving execution problems is to bring the organization's "stakeholder owners" together and have them work together as an **alignment council** on the *execution gaps*. With an alignment council, everyone sees their success tied to the successes of others. As such, alignment councils have been shown to enhance collaboration, improve decision making and creative problem solving and, most importantly, break down the barriers to cooperation without having to reorganize.

An example of an alignment council is shown in Figure 3.

Figure 3

ALIGNMENT COUNCIL

Question 18

If the company is considering a merger, acquisition or joint venture, has it put in place all of the systems necessary to enhance its post-deal integration?

The problems of M&As and joint ventures are many. So much so that, according to Professor Michael Porter of the Harvard Business School, between 55–86% of all M&As are not successful and many are complete failures (see Exhibit 5). The most glaring issue contributing to their failure appears to be the inability of any two organizations—regardless of their size and/or relatedness—to integrate their cultures. And it is this failure that undermines all of the positive aspects of the firms' decision to join forces in the first place.

For instance, in one company it was well known in advance of an acquisition that the reputation of the target firm's management team and corporate culture could be a major problem to successful integration. The M&A was desirable because the acquirer believed it was the shortest route to obtaining an emerging technology needed to meet changing market conditions. While the Board first considered removing the management team of the target organization, it changed that condition after the investment bankers indicated that there would be no deal if the management team were not brought "aboard" as a whole. The acquisition then proceeded with the acquiring firm and its Board taking none of the steps suggested in this publication to align the two organizations' existing organizational arrangements with the "planned combined strategy." As a consequence, numerous *execution gaps* appeared and the acquisition was subsequently judged to be a disaster which almost brought down the acquiring organization!

Directors therefore should use the strategy execution questions provided here to probe management on any proposed M&A or joint venture as part of its due diligence. While M&As are sold on the basis of supposedly bolstering the product pipeline, broadening technology, gaining a geographical "toe-hold", etc., the success of any M&A ultimately will depend on whether or not the management team is prepared to address all of the strategy execution issues raised above that might undermine the successful realization of perceived synergies.

Unfortunately, due diligence activities typically do not cover the strategy execution issues addressed in this book. Accordingly, Boards are encouraged especially to consider a pre- and/or post-M&A *Strategy Execution Audit*™ to find out where any *execution gaps* may be, and the options for closing them. In addition, experience has shown that companies are well advised to constitute an alignment council to assure successful integration of the two firms.

Exhibit 5

Acquisition program analysis:

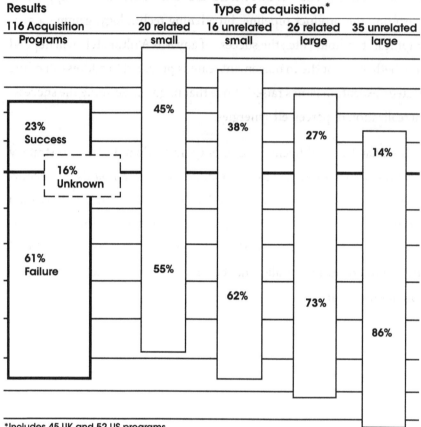

Results	Type of acquisition*			
116 Acquisition Programs	20 related small	16 unrelated small	26 related large	35 unrelated large

23% Success

16% Unknown

61% Failure

45%

55%

38%

62%

27%

73%

14%

86%

*Includes 45 UK and 52 US programs,
excludes 19 (16%) with unknown results

Question 19

Has the Board allowed sufficient time for the strategy to be executed?

The successful execution of a strategy is, without a doubt, the most complex and time consuming aspect of an organization's strategic management processes. Crafting a well thought out strategy can occur within a relatively short period of time. But turning the aims and aspirations of any strategy into reality often takes careful and considerable effort that always needs to be well coordinated throughout the entire enterprise. Depending upon the magnitude of any change in the strategy, the execution of it may take up to several years! Moreover, because conditions in both the external and internal environments are always changing, past decisions become subject to constant review and possible modification. Boards, therefore, need to seriously consider the time frame in which the execution of their organization's strategy is realistically feasible.

Of course, all Boards and their managements want to execute their organization's strategy quickly. But in their haste for performance results, they should not let the reality of the organization's circumstances (i.e. its readiness for execution) blind them to the time required. Indeed, as the late Chairman Mao Tse Tung once observed: "The beginning of wisdom is the recognition and acceptance of reality." Despite his commitment to communism, he provides excellent advice for impatient capitalists.

Xerox would have done well to heed his words. At one point in the company's history, management decided, simultaneously to a) collapse its 53 call centers into just 3 within a single year; and b) to change its decades old "country specific" sales force into one that was globally oriented and based on industry categories. For the latter move, management also proposed that a "series of short training courses" be initiated to help re-orient the sales force. Both decisions were reviewed and quickly approved by the Board. Both quickly failed. Not because they were necessarily the wrong moves to make but because neither management nor the Board saw the problems inherent in the execution time frame. As a result, the CEO was fired.

It is therefore strongly recommended that, notwithstanding the tremendous pressure in today's environment for quick action and quick results, Boards temper their hastiness with caution and diligence. They especially need to spend sufficient time finding out what it really takes for effective strategy execution to happen and not give short shrift to the reality of the timelines truly required. Once completed, the "realistic" execution timeline should be aggressively communicated to the organization's key stakeholders to counter any short-term pressures for quick results.

Question 20

Has the Board made an assessment of management's ability to lead strategy execution?

As noted previously, research has found that most involuntary CEO departures are because a Board determined that their CEO could not execute the firm's strategy. However, research from the University of California, Irvine[12], found that *successors hired by the Board often did not improve things substantially!* That is, there was no significant improvement in operating earnings or stock performance with a new CEO. Why? Because the Boards studied did not thoroughly gauge the ability of their new CEO to successfully execute the strategy any better than they had for the previous CEO. Moreover, experience suggests that when facing such circumstances, the preferred *modus operandi* of most Boards and their CEOs is simply to retreat back to the drawing board to find a better strategy!

Boards therefore would be wise both to assess their current and any potential CEO (and perhaps all corporate officers) on their ability to lead the execution of their organization's strategy and to have a *Strategy Execution Audit™, to assist them.* Such an evaluation would help the Board determine whether coaching and counseling – using the services of a qualified consultant -- might be more appropriate than simply firing the CEO. It would also help the Board determine if any potential successor has the ability to improve things.

Interestingly, while there are many questionnaires on personality and management style, as well as ones related to a person's ability to develop good strategy, there have been none designed to address an executive's

---

12   http://hbr.org/2002/12/holes-at-the-top-why-ceo-firings-backfire/ar/1

strengths and weaknesses in strategy execution – until now. The authors developed a unique assessment questionnaire, displayed in Appendix 2, which focuses specifically on assessing a leader's capability in this area. We encourage Boards to have all key leaders in their companies complete it as well as to use it to evaluate new key executive hires. The resulting information should provide good insight into both the culture of the company and the ability of its leaders to execute the corporate strategy with excellence.

Post Script Question:

You've asked the 20 Questions, now what?

No Director or Board should be surprised if the answers to the 20 Questions listed above are NOT satisfactory. This is because, as has been stated several times above, the vast majority of companies do not execute their strategy well. Yet Boards obviously want to help their companies succeed, not just in terms of having the right strategy, but also in its execution. The two strategy execution tools described in

Appendix 1 and 2 describe the immediate steps that can be taken to set a company on its path to Execution Excellence and make it a part of the 10% Club that successfully overcomes its execution problems.

Appendix 1

The Strategy Execution Audit™

The authors *Strategy Execution Audit™* is the fastest way for a Board to find out where execution problems exist. The process steps and essential components of the audit are displayed in Figure 4.

Figure 4
The Strategy Execution Audit™

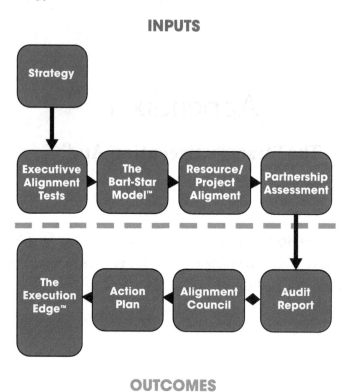

INPUTS

Strategy

Executivve Alignment Tests

The Bart-Star Model™

Resource/ Project Aligment

Partnership Assessment

The Execution Edge™

Action Plan

Alignment Council

Audit Report

OUTCOMES

As Figure 4 indicates, a firm's *formally approved strategy* forms the starting point for the *Strategy Execution Audit™*. We assume that you have already given a lot of thought and consideration to developing a good one.

As a first step, the *Strategy Execution Audit™ looks* for strategic alignment amongst the senior leadership team because if this group is not in line with the organization's strategy, it is doubtful the rest of the employees will be. Ironically, Boards often assume from the CEO's statements to them that this alignment exists. In our private interviews with a firm's senior leaders, however, we typically find that the C-suite is not aligned.

The next step is to assess the state of strategic alignment among the organization's business unit and functional leaders.

Using Chris Bart's exclusive *"Bart-Star Model"*(see Figure 2), the Audit team then assess the degree to which the organizational structures, systems, policies and procedures found in the functional and business units are being used to coordinate and control employee activities with the strategy. The Audit team further test for alignment of the organization's resources to make sure that only those projects and initiatives that contribute to the strategy's realization get funded.

The *Strategy Execution Audit™* also includes a unique evaluation of external partners such as PR/advertising agencies and supply chain partners who interface with customers. The Audit team does this to determine if they are executing appropriately on *your* strategy.

The first major deliverable of the *Strategy Execution Audit™* is a report that identifies not only where the execution gaps exist *and their ranked order*, but also how to correct them to enhance *Execution Excellence™*.

The Audit team then uses this report to help the company create an Alignment Council™, pioneered by Elliot Schreiber, comprised of key internal and external stakeholders. Using the Audit Report, the Council develops Execution Action Plans that close the identified execution gaps and finally deliver the *Execution Edge™*.

The *Strategy Execution Audit™* is a proven way for a Board, CEO or business unit head to quickly determine where strategic execution is breaking down, or could break down, and how to correct any gaps in the shortest period of time in the most practical manner.

Appendix 2

Are You and the Members of Your Team *Strategy Execution Leaders?*

As you complete the following *Strategy Execution Leadership Assessment Questionnaire*™, please think about how you work and have worked in the past moving from strategy to execution. Average your scores for each of the strategy execution leadership skills listed below. As a general guide, scores averaging below "4" should be considered problematic and identified as areas for improvement.

To what extent do you:	Rarely					Routinely				
	1	2	3	4	5	6	7	8	9	10
Vision										
Establish a higher vision to which the organization should strive?										
Articulate clearly and unambiguously what the organization will look like and will have accomplished when it successfully executes its strategy?										
Communication and Organizational Awareness										
Personally take responsibility for articulating the strategy clearly and precisely to everyone in the organization?										
Obtain feedback that assures that the strategy has been heard, understood and remembered by all?										
Culture										
Assure that all line managers and functional heads know about, understand, and live the values and associated behaviors required to support the strategy?										
Establish rewards and recognition for those who help the organization succeed through demonstrably living the values?										
Capability										
Assure the qualifications and abilities required of employees to implement the strategy—including effective training, recruitment and termination appropriate?										

To what extent do you:	Rarely					Routinely				
	1	2	3	4	5	6	7	8	9	10
Capability (continued)										
Assure that the core competencies and resources support strategy execution?										
Integration										
Address conflicting interests and actions of stakeholders?										
Break down silos that undermine successful collaboration and execution?										
Ensure all functional units are highly integrated in their mutual quest to execute the strategy?										
Ensure all external partners are aligned with the strategy in their execution efforts?										
Establish rewards and recognition for those who help the organization succeed through cooperation and collaboration?										
Feedback and Recognition										
Assure that all line managers and functional leaders show how the strategy is executed through their units and vice versa?										
Give performance enhancing reviews rather than negative, blaming ones?										
Celebrate execution successes?										

Authors' Biographies

Chris Bart, Ph.D. FCPA

Chris Bart, Ph.D., FCPA is the world's leading expert on mission and vision statement effectiveness. He is also a Co-Founder, Principal and Lead Professor of The Directors College at McMaster University, Canada's first university accredited corporate director certification program. Bart has authored the 10 year Canadian business best seller *A Tale of Two Employees and the Person Who Wanted to Lead Them* (2003), as well as the widely acclaimed publications *20 Essential Questions Corporate Directors Should Ask About Strategy* (2012) and *The Mission Driven Hospital* (2013).

Through his pioneering research and teachings, Bart has become highly sought after by organizations seeking to develop vision and mission statements that get results. His practical approach for bringing mission statements to life has inspired business leaders and audiences around the world.

As a Professor of Strategy and Governance at McMaster University's DeGroote School of Business, Bart has published over 160 articles, cases and reviews. He currently serves as Associate Editor of the *International Journal of Business Governance and Ethics.*

Bart has been awarded the Ontario Chamber of Commerce "Outstanding Business Achievement Award for Corporate Governance," the Hamilton Chamber of Commerce "HR Hero Award," the United Way "Chairman's Award," the HRPA 2011 "Summit Award for Corporate Governance & Strategic Leadership," and McMaster's "Innovation Award." For his research, he has received both the McMaster Research Recognition Award and its Theory to Practice Award. A highly regarded lecturer, Bart has received both the "Outstanding Undergraduate Business Professor" and "MBA Professor of the Year" awards on multiple occasions. He has also won "The President's Award for Teaching Excellence", McMaster's highest teaching award – which made him the most decorated professsor at the DeGroote School. In 2009, his CA designation was elevated to FCA (Fellow of the Institute of Chartered Accountants). And in 2012, Bart was the recipient of the Queen Elizabeth II Diamond Jubilee Medal for service to Canada.

Over the years, Bart has been invited to consult with numerous institutions throughout the world, including South Africa, Switzerland, the United Kingdom, Australia, the Czech Republic and China.

Bart is listed in *Canadian Who's Who*. He is currently a member of the Board of Terra Firma Capital Corporation (TII.V) and its Audit Committee. He is a past Director of St. Joseph's Hospital, the Harshman Foundation, the Canadian Foundation for Education and Research on Finance, the United Way, and Eagle Precision Technologies (a former TSE listed company) where he chaired its Compensation Committee.

Elliot S. Schreiber, Ph.D.

Elliot S. Schreiber, Ph.D. is Co-Founder of the Directors College, a joint venture between McMaster University and The Conference Board, and Canada's first university accredited corporate director certification program. He is one of those rare individuals who has moved seamlessly within the corporate executive suite, academia and consulting. He has gained an international reputation as one of the most experienced and knowledgeable experts in strategy execution, with a particular focus on market strategies, including brand and reputation management.

Schreiber began his career as a pharmaceutical salesman, and then, after receiving his Ph.D. from Penn State University, became a professor at the University of Delaware. In 1980, he left the academic world to join the DuPont Company at its headquarters in Wilmington, DE, where the Chairman asked him to develop the market strategy for the company's move into pharmaceutical and electronic products. His work led the company to reorganize its businesses to gain greater synergies and market focus. In 1986, he joined Bayer Corporation in Pittsburgh, PA, where until 1995 he served as Senior Vice President with responsibility for the company's North American corporate marketing and communications. At Bayer, he led the company's rebranding efforts when it changed from a holding company to an operating company.

From 1995-1999, Schreiber was Chief Marketing and Communications Officer at Nortel Networks, where he was in charge of all marketing and communications globally, and chaired the company's global Sales and Marketing Council. From 1999-2001, he was Managing Partner and Chief Operating Officer of Digital 4Sight, an international e-business consulting firm based in Toronto, On. He and his partners sold the firm in 2001 and he returned to teaching and consulting.

From 2001-2004, he was Industry Professor at the DeGroote School of Business, McMaster University. From 2006–2007, he was Senior Advisor to the Reputation Institute, New York, where he created their consulting business plan. From 2008–2012, he was Clinical Professor of Marketing and Executive Director of the Centre for Corporate Reputation Management, at the LeBow College of Business, Drexel University, Philadelphia. He also has been a visiting professor or guest lecturer at a number of other universities in the U.S. and Canada. He is a past Board member of Aprimo, dna13 Inc., ConvoNation, United Way and the National Conference of Christians and Jews.

Schreiber is widely sought as a speaker at international business and academic conferences. He has written numerous articles and book chapters on brand, reputation and reputation risk. In addition, his blogging has gained popularity as a source for business writers internationally.

Schreiber holds a B.A. from the University of Delaware and a Ph.D. from Penn State University. He holds both U.S. and Canadian citizenship.

CPSIA information can be obtained at www.ICGtesting.com
Printed in the USA
LVOW02s1415160415

434860LV00014B/207/P